BLUE

LIKE

APPLES

BLUE

LIKE

APPLES

Rasma Haidri

REBEL SATORI PRESS
New Orleans & New York

Published in the United States of America by
Rebel Satori Press
www.rebelsatoripress.com

Book design: Sven Davisson

Paperback ISBN: 978-1-60864-276-2

Library of Congress Control Number: 2023938510

for Veronica ~ lylmlu

Acknowledgments

Grateful acknowledgement is made to the editors of the following publications in which versions of the following poems first appeared:

Action, Spectacle: "Whole"
Antiphon: "Skype from America"
Ice Floe: "The Theory of Everything" and "Stand-In"
Galway Review: "24/10/03"
Lavender Review: "Stopping by the Sea Before Catching Your
              Flight"
Popcorn Farm: "Wolf"
Queer Around the World, Too: "Pride"
Sycamore Review: "The Passion"
Young Ravens Literary Review: "Currents" and "Trust"

Contents

I.

II.

III.

I.

Valentine's Eve

A throng turns out in this arctic town
to protest the U.S. assault on Iraq.

I see you watching me in the crowd,
shouts like gunshot: PEACE! NOW!
cowboy Bush lynched in effigy, his
flag on fire, his country

no longer mine.
I have none, no one,
not even you speak my language,
my mother tongue mute
after the city I loved fell,
twice-buried beneath towers of dust.

You slip from khaki pockets
a pencil stub, small red notebook.
I wonder what you write, why I
didn't even think to bring a journal.

The crowd roils around me,
a snagged branch in a surging flood.
My husband, carrying one daughter,
whispers: "I looked for you,
then saw your tiger-striped hair."

On the brink of invasion,
I have no idea how the world will change.

Pomes

Late spring's liquid nighttime sun
plays lava-lamp over stained glass,
as overtones swell our choir to a resounding host
in the cathedral crossing.

At break I take to a corner, clutching pencil
and black-bound journal. "Are you writing poems?"
The voice is yours, the alto who insists
on speaking English, claims she's British,
though I suspect another Norwegian
wanting language practice.

I stare, recalling the winter-long polar night,
what locals call the Dark Time—depressive,
poemless months when doctors and my husband
said I'd feel better if I'd write. I said I'd write
if I felt better, sure I never would.

But now—relentless, baffling light
lays molten rainbow halos over our heads,
as you say, "I've written some, maybe one day
you could tell me if they're any good?"

I nod, bewildered by *POMES* on the spine
of your forest green binder. Can't you spell?
Or is it an anagram, a metaphor,

POMES itself a poem I almost fathom,
like your bold colored mismatched socks,
like the rogue sun at ten pm forging from colored glass
an alchemy of light.

Second Choice

You invite me to the movies,
adding, "Bring your husband!"
Your therapist suggested
you socialize, and Anne the soprano
couldn't come.

We see *Gangs of New York.*
He on my left, gobbles a jumbo chocolate bar.
You on my right, slip me a sour-feet-gummy.
"My favorite," you whisper.

Tart sugar numbs my tongue
as I suck piquant juices from tiny toes,
painful, pleasure, strangeness, delight.

Pencil

Sopranos and altos rise,
fold chairs, music stands.
Rehearsal's over, but I
can't find my pencil,
the expensive one I
know I should never take
out of the house.

I pretend calm, linger, lift
cushions, dig in pockets, purse,
search the folds of my notes.

You pause, "What is it?"
"I lost my pencil." I cringe,
chagrined, what fool
brings a gold-plated Parker to choir?

You shout to the others:
"Let's help find her pencil!"
but only you stay
in the hollow church, moving
pews, patting down papers,
wheeling aside the grand piano
while I trudge the aisles,
eyes on the floor.

The surprise is not
the gleam of the pencil, glimpsed
reclining like a streamlined spacecraft
on the speckled tile. No, it's how you smile,
radiating relief

as you wrap me in a hug
so free of yourself,
I'm stunned such joy can exist
on my behalf.

Turning Earth

Because you are English,
I ask you to help me fix up my yard
where, with a hand spade, I unearthed
a black stone large enough to sit on.

I picture a rock garden oasis
in the snail-infested lawn
where my husband felled the lone tree,
and nothing grows but moss

and legions of spiky triffids
I tried all spring to cull. The ones
I missed grew long, unearthly
stems tipped with hoary, fist-sized
buds that split and burst papery red.

Icelandic poppies, you name them,
then unload plants you lugged
on the bus: *lemon thyme, saxifrage,*
clematis—little did I know,
you come from a line of bona fide
English gardeners.

You send me to buy a garden fork,
then turn soil, cordon compost,
carve steps into the sloping lawn,

point to the wall my husband erected
where you would plant wild
strawberries to drape over the stone

and for a moment, I dare believe
an Eden conjured by your hand.

Art History

I haven't heard of Frida Kahlo,
but you say it will be an arty film,
so I don't bother to bring my husband.

We slouch in the front row
as smoky, androgynous Frida
fills the screen, leading a woman
in a pivoting, riveting tango—
when she kisses her we both
gasp—you hand me your bag
of sugar-coated feet.

Afterwards, at Café Kafka,
I offer more than once the space
beside me on the couch,
but you don't look up from rummaging
in your backpack,
mumble that your wing chair is fine.

The lukewarm latte
is also disappointing.

Three months later, you will tell me
it was on this night
you decided not to move
from Bodø to Kristiansand,

just finish your degree there,
and return.

I will smile.
I will not ask why.

Means to Fly

It may be your therapy homework,
but no one has ever cooked me curry
and laid such a table: emerald rectangular plates,
woven purple mats, porcelain brocade cups,
matte pewter knives and forks.

You pour from a Bodum you fitted
with a tailored paisley cozy,
and I love for the first time
drinking coffee bitter and black,
with a rough shard of dark chocolate,
not milky brown squares I break
along prescribed lines.

Why don't I know how to make curry?
And why is that bejeweled red silk
tapestry stitched with gold
on your wall, not mine?
It could have lain on the forehead
of a maharaja's elephant
in the India of my father's boyhood,
before the British, from which you descend,
carved up the subcontinent.

A woman's purple ceramic mask
hangs from the ceiling, bound in gold mesh,

a centerpiece that broke,
so you hung it out of the way.

I say, "That's art!"
You start clearing dishes, "You think?"

I think I have discovered you,
opened a window on your soul.
The woman didn't break, she broke free,
and now she's on her way—where do women go
when they leave?

"It's art," I repeat. "Don't you know
you're an artist?"

You shrug, mention a painting
you gave your mother,
a jungle mural for your ex-lover's son,
a calendar encircling your therapist's office,
made of your footprints,
and those of a little girl you saw
playing in the road.

I ask to see photos. You say,
"Why would I take photos? (To show me?
I inwardly cry.) Each piece
went to the one it was for."

I can't account for my anger, envy,

the loss I feel—a mad, covetous desire
to wrench from the hands of strangers
everything you gave them,
all I wish you had given me.

Trace Evidence

I have never sent or received
a text message, till I get this:

Watcher doon?

I stare at the screen, unable to interpret
your British slang, until I read it aloud.
I type:

Not much, and you?

I'm writing.

What are you writing?

Things I want to remember.

Remember me?
I dare not jest: a grocery list?
I type:

Me too.

What are you writing?

Things I want to remember.

I'll show you mine if you show me yours.

I can't,
don't answer.

Find out what you need then let me know.

I need—to breathe.
Drop my phone.

Con Brio

The choir sings, Yule. Take one. Take two.
Waiting for sound check, I reach to return
a book you lent me, *The First Miracle*,

about a Roman boy watching Joseph, Mary, and donkey
enter the stable. "Yes, I liked it," I say,
still not sure I did, or why you, a heathen, would.

In the instant you take the book and say, "You look well,
I'm glad you're no longer ill," I see blood-crusted slash lines
on your arm, and look away—How can you be glad for me?

During break, you splay your hand atop a piano,
rapidly stabbing a pushpin between fingers,
just missing each stretched skin web,

a kind of Russian roulette,
as you tell me of a letter from your mother
you don't dare open,

a professor scoffing: "No one gets the top exam grade,"
but you did, in voice, singing,
Sometimes I Feel Like a Motherless Child.

I want to reach and stop your stabbing,
but don't dare interrupt. Or leave.

Or ask if you're crazy.

I stay, because three months after 9-11, I've tried every
Norwegian-FDA-approved Happy-Pill
without success—but you see me, your words generous

as your arms are self-harming,
fresh cuts perpendicular to gnarled white scars,
like perforations indicating where to tear.

Craven

I skip my class
in Adult Dyslexic Word Processing,
to drop by for a chat,
as if spending three hours free
from husband and children
is an ordinary thing,

but I'm breathless as you open the door.
I've never seen
a woman smile before.

You're just stepping out to fetch an ingredient
I've not heard of and can't pronounce.
"Come in! Wait here, we'll eat."

You leave rice steaming on the stove,
and on the table—your journal
propped open, your cursive
covering white pages,
like the black marble inscriptions
on the Taj Mahal.

Who are you, so unguarded
against the likes of me?
Don't you know I would steal,
break in, plunder, take

what I want, need?

I glance at the door,
gauge distance. I could pretend to be
checking the rice if you appear
before I have ravaged the pages
to find what I crave

but don't dare look for, could not bear
not finding—my name
in your hand.

24/10/03

Sometime in July, I buy a carton
of fake coffee cream destined to expire
on a date you will no longer live here.

It fits my hand like a grenade
missing its pin.

Wolf

We take my daughter and her friend
to see *Wolf Summer* at the movies,
and like a nervous teen, I wonder
if I will get to sit by you, and whether
we'll dare to hold hands, or touch arms
on the armrest, as even strangers
sometimes do—but we don't,
so I cry real tears at the end
with the eight-year-olds.

The next day you text: *I missed
being able to hold your hand,*
and I can't breathe for the joy
of you, a woman like me, wanting
a woman like me.

My daughter climbs onto her parents' bed
to show she's making a book:

> WOLF.
> The wolf parents meet another grown-up
> wolf and they all become friends then one
> of them asks the others if they can all live
> together and the wolf cubs cheer and wag
> their tails and howl because of course the
> answer is Yes!

"That's nice, Honey," I say,
and don't look at her father
who is smiling, eyebrow raised,
because he has already proposed: I can have you
if he can have you, too.

I lock myself in the bathroom,
dry-heave howls,
unsure of my affliction.

Casablanca Remix

After the choir's summer party
in the airport control tower,
we linger in the parking lot,
my flapping scarf unfurls
to muss your hair.

An alto's boxy Volvo
waits to drive me home.
"Well, go on then," you say,
in your clipped British tongue.

You're right. I should go home,
to husband and children and bed.
I should rein in my scarf,
walk right past your pocketed hands,
as violins croon and cameras pan
to make you a dot on the tarmac,
me a smudge in the car window
receding along a cliffside road.

But I am the heroine
who does not leave.

Here's the close-up:
me, in a flapping scarf,
you, in a Burberry coat.

Background:
a blurry yellow Volvo
gears up, exits scene.

Pan-out:
we turn toward town,
follow a maze of cobbled streets.

Not yet arm in arm,
the heroine not yet brave,
but in your apartment,
fingers graze over a cup of tea.

Later you walk me to the stop,
our two cold hands
in one woolen pocket.

I board the Late Bus,
smile at the rowdy drunks,
then at you, tall and solid
on the street, smiling at me.

Fade-out: bus.
Cue-in: oboe.

To be continued…
superimposed on the screen.

II.

Eve of Departure

I sit on the edge of your couch,
a twin mattress you covered
in paisley and damasked cushions,

you, on the floor, lean back, hand me
over your shoulder, the liniment
your sister sends from London,

good for sore gardening muscles.
"Would you mind rubbing some in?"
I watch you unbutton your shirt

as you warn, "Keep it out
of your eyes, and afterwards be sure
to wash your hands."

I lift a pungent dollop in each palm,
as if supplicating a goddess,
as you say, "Perhaps it's easier

if I move these a bit, if you don't mind."
"No," I say, watching bra straps
fall in slow loops

stop halfway to your elbow,
level with lacy cups
shadowing your breasts,

a wine-red bra so surprising
under bleach-died shirt, so girly-girly
above khaki men's shorts.

My hands fit your shoulders,
like they don't his. Perhaps, I never wanted
to open them wide enough.

Now, they want to follow the falling
bra straps along your arms,
pull you into my knees.

I want to lay my head
on your mopsey curls,
hold you.

We part with our usual sisterly kiss.

II.

New message, read now?
I press, *Yes*, one hand on the steering wheel,
read: *Remember, wash your hands!*

I lay the phone on the seat, grieving
this practical text, wanting—something,
not this.
Not what's next.

He'll expect me to come to bed.
No, I'll say
when he asks if it's a burden,
but it is.

I would buy him his dream home,
a shack in Hawaii, send him off happy,
then welcome you in—

you, me, my daughters playing and laughing
as women do in a house brimming
with useless items of senseless beauty,

sofas with cushions, shelves with books,
tables decked with our garden bouquets,
crumpets and scones we bake
from tattered recipes.

III.

I pull into the garage, check my phone,
send you: *OK*, with smiley,
enter my home,

hands closed in loose fists.
I don't look at them as I wash,
nor at my face in the mirror.

I look at nothing,
and when they are dry,
my hands smell of nothing, too.

Cold Comfort

I.

I sit where strong sun spotlights me
in a wing seat,
as the jet crosses your British Isles,

war planes swoop on overhead screens,
rising in victory,
or plummeting to oblivion.

I order my first ever cognac,
practice sipping it,
as you did yours.

II.

I write love poems, in Norwegian,
so the brandy-on-ice woman beside me,
in glitter-jeans, designer-frames, sequined-shirt,
can't read our secret.

But she's watching fighter planes morph into Kurt Cobain,
her red nails tapping his beat
on the fold-down tray, gray head banging along,
so I wonder if she's a retired rocker,

or maybe choir director.

She doesn't notice me, my pen scratching
at a poem,
as careful cognac-sips scorch my throat.

III.

I order coffee to counteract the cognac surge,
but "coffee" is a pale, tepid wash
in a white styrofoam cup,
evoking my mother's instant
mixed with tap water and powdered cream.

If you were here I might bear the cognac,
in tune with you,
and this globe-traveling, grunge-loving woman,
so alien to the likes of my mother,
or me.

But I am alone.
I spoil the cognac,
swirl it into the coffee swill.

Somewhere over the Atlantic,
the stewardess removes it.

Silent Tattoo

The same sun shines on us both,
you in bed on the Norwegian coast,
me searching a California desert
to find you a rock
where none seem to exist.

Only Amazon-size cactus blooms,
sister-cacti to the prickly blades
you nurture on your windowsill,
where the surreal arctic sun
shines in at two am.

Sleeping, pacific, do you dream me,
half a world away?

I can't quite conjure your face,
wonder if I've invented us
the way my Norse ancestors invented time
under summer's nighttime sun.

Between my throat and t-shirt top,
is the spot your warm fingertips pressed,
indelible, invisible, a brand still burning.

Skype from America

Birds chirp
in a foreign tongue,
and even children
sound like canaries
to you—who cannot feel
I am trying
to nudge your fingers
from your eyes
with the arrow
of my cursor.

Pride

When the Parisian Gay Pride parade
pauses outside Hotel Lyon,
I rush to join,

waving my 35 mm SLR in one hand,
notebook in the other,
hoping the beige macramé skirt-set
you mended with an ivory remnant,
passes as journalist attire,

because I'm not one of them:
these pink-tutu prancing men,
pipe-smoking women in lumberjack shirts
and steel-toed boots.

I break through the crowd, *Excusez-moi!*
snapping faux photos of clouds,
then fall in line toward La Bastille.

When Florence, the woman on my right,
asks if I do this each year, I dissemble,
Je suis touriste,

tell her I'm from north of the Arctic Circle
where no pride parades exist,
though I don't know if that's true,

only I wouldn't be caught dead in one,
what would people think? I'd lose my job,
be put in jail, get stoned on the street.

Even here, I fear the parade will make *The New York Times*,
centering me in a front-page photo,
arresting the hearts of my Wisconsin aunts.

Florence says she's seen Oslo Pride on TV,
says Scandinavians are known for sexual liberation.
I say I only live there, I'm American.

On Rue des Trois Soeurs, she asks if I'm gay,
and I tell her I have you, *ma petite amie*,
unsure what word describes you
in any language.

My husband's fine with it, I lie,
as if we three have worked it out,
as if you and I know love
the way this woman surely does.

At Place de la Concorde,
I tell her what's true: my husband understands
you are impossible not to love.

She smiles, and I know I belong
in this harlequin parade.
People should see a woman like me,

of no certain age, a housewife, teacher, neighbor,
just an ordinary woman clad in beige,
in love with a woman,
sea-changed.

The tide sweeps me further from the curb,
from any ground,
as my camera prop dangles,
notebook forgotten,
I turn to face clamoring reporters,
telling myself—don't be afraid.

Seen

Detroit, Michigan, 1956,
a boy stood at twilight
in the empty playground,
back to the creaking swings,
knocking his head
against a galvanized post.

No one took him in her arms,
not his mother, if he had one,
not my mother, at her window,
not me, not yet born.

My mother told this fragment of story,
a scene replaying,
the sky always gray, cold
as the pole he tried for solace.

I begin to understand the reach
through flesh, bone, steel
to feel the pain
that feels like being seen.

You, age five,
in cotton sheet and foil halo,
waited in vain
to be seen by your mother

who never came.

You, age three,
knocked down (forehead split
on stone) by your mother
demonstrating: *That's how it feels*,
after you accidentally
knocked over your sister.

You, age thirty-three,
on the lam from psych ward A,
nabbed by police,
your father flew in, *There there.*
Chin up. It'll all be the same
in a hundred years.

Your mother didn't come,
or send a card,
but a year or ten later,
still ignoring your scars,
she said what you needed then
was to come to her arms.

I praise the science teacher
who asked, "Do you know you have a constellation
on your cheek?"

At thirteen,
you felt seen among stars.

Solstice

My husband hangs up the phone
after a Christmas call to Uchi, his once-girlfriend,

then hugs me, saying,
"Thank you for a wonderful life."

Did something dawn on him?
Is he going somewhere?

"Goodbye?" I say.
He doesn't hear.

I say, "You're welcome."
He says, "What?"

The sun in winter
turns away from us, leaves.

The long polar night
a trial separation.

Trust

I kneel in the attic,
next to a box of little girl dresses,
feeling our impending goodbye.
No brain, I am only heart
and skin and breathing,
        staring at nothing,
not even an imagined
Kristiansand—
        till I see
in the flashlight beam,
a world of dust, swirling chaos,
specks like planets
flung from orbit,
        massing, revolving, returning,
splitting into twos, threes,
lonely ones—
        and I know
I orchestrated
this fugue of spheres.
        As I watch,
everything changes:
dust specks settle
into one flow,
from solos to chorus,
        and this, too, I know
I conduct.

Stopping by the Sea Before Catching Your Flight

We stay so long in the car
the windows steam over,
making a curtain that hides us
from wind-blown barn, rain clouds, gulls.
Mjelle's red sand just visible
through the cleared circle
made in the window fog
by the mass of your brown hair.

A Woman's Cycle

How dare we think one month matters?
Love, don't tell me the limits you see.
Soon twenty-eight days
will be twenty-eight months,
and we will have a room, a home, a place to be
where strawberries you have yet to plant,
will be ripe and full and sweet.

My mother wouldn't let this be.
Once, at an interstate oasis, she pointed
to a glowering, narrow-eyed waitress:
"See that woman, she's a lesbian."

From across the room, the wretch cast her evil eye.
I said, "Maybe, she's just an unhappy,
overworked single mother." But my mother said,
"No. She has the look of a lesbian, that tough,
threatening, I-will-devour-you look."
She hoped I would be afraid.

Love, I love to lie on cushions of red brocade,
run my finger along your nape,
where once you said I must not touch,
or you would have to eat me up.

Come, love, I'm not afraid.

Let us consume one another, not woman, not man,
just lover and beloved,
because love consumed will phoenix-rise,
love begets love,
one of many things my mother denied.

The Theory of Everything

I read today that quarks,
building blocks of neutrons,
(I imagine them modeled
in your socks' bright colors),

behave as free particles
in proximity,
tangoing in asymptotic freedom,

yet, as they separate,
the force of their bond
strengthens—the farther away,
the tighter the hold,

so, unlike gravity,
which weakens to infinity
by an inverse square law
(the reason stars shine dimly),

the Law of Quantum Chromodynamics
proves by mathematics
that a quark in Bodø binds unalterably
to a quark in Kristiansand,
not a neutrino of love
lost to distance.

The Gift

What was your gift, today?
you write in a letter.
Mine was a little boy
walking one foot on the curb,
one in the gutter,
for a city block.

Your expectation of daily gifts,
as simple as a child walking unfazed
in two worlds at once, balancing
on unequal terrain, not a worry to spare
for impossibility,
is my gift.

III.

Stroll in Kristiansand

Like Gertrude and Alice, they walk
side by side through the park,
a pair of old ladies talking non-stop,
heads bobbing above many-colored coats.

Will I be her, the silver page-boy
pushing a walker? Will you be the one
in green shoes and purple socks,
leaning on a bird-claw cane?

They pause, lift pearl-strung
spectacles, examine flowers, gates,
a tree's girth, gesture at a building
that's there, a fountain that's not.

Giggling, shoulders shaking,
the old ladies whisper-shout:
The sparrow had an ice cream mustache!
Acupuncture with a capital A!

It is a silliness only
their shared life makes sense of.
We giggle, too.
                    I take your hand,
reciting Donne: "Come live with me,
and be my love…"

your kiss is my yes,
as the old couple *hem hem, hum hum,*
passes arm in arm,
tottering on.

Liftoff

I would show you
this white ocean of cloud,

        not gray as doubt
        seen from underneath,

sunlit—a bright-white bed pierced
by granite peaks called Seven Sisters,

        a mountain range
        of hefty female haunches,

marking your way back north,
to all the uncharted

        surface and depth
        we have yet to explore.

Never So Free

I ask if you miss your ex,
and you say you miss the clawfoot tub,
his acupuncture and deep massage,
the, First-to-the-Sofa! after dinner game,
hiking across the Lofoten islands,
the delight of sitting naked on a log to pee,
the remote beach where once little boys
watched from dunes as the two of you
sunbathed nude.

I have never been so free.
At twenty-one, on my hike-the-Arctic
honeymoon, I refused to skinny dip
in a mountain lake—what if people
in an airplane could see?

You say, "Not him, I miss
the things we did together."

I nod, envious.
I miss the things you did together, too.

Stand-In

An emasculated peacock
felt your longing
through the wire fence.
He quickened,
eager to show you
his beautiful erection.
But of his plumage,
the only remaining feathers
were small, shimmering scales
quivering with yearning,
his desire straining
to cry out,
fan you.

Mjelle

Red sand granules
drop one by one
from my fingers over your arm,
not to bury, but awaken you,
at Mjelle.

We lie beneath grassy crags,
where grazing sheep look like
broken-off pieces of cliff.
To them we look like pieces of beach,
mer-creatures washed ashore,
wet and panting in new air,
at Mjelle.

Warships passed, but no map
showed a reason to stop,
so soldiers never saw this garnet sand,
the stones that would've made them kneel
and drop their guns,
at Mjelle.

Find me a truth stone,
I'll find you one.
Our footprints leading to the car
will write our names,
at Mjelle.

Perspective

I peer close to the paper
            to see from your eyes
how the pencil moved,
                your hand sketching
these lines at these angles,
           one long and straight,
               one lying on its side,
         the pencil tip
      drawing dimension
from a flat plane,
        raising memory,
           constructing insight,
disproving doubt,
       the way Descartes described
          knowledge as geometry,
the world a sum
      of straight lines
        roof lines,
           power lines,
              all V's and A's
like letters in your name,
               and on each housetop
        where antennae pitch,
     a single chimney-cube
              marks the hearth
          beneath each roof I saw

framed in your kitchen window,
over your shoulder, in our embrace.

Antique Whites

Twenty-one years ago,
when you were nineteen and in love
with a woman for the first time,
I was birthing my first child.

Her father, my husband,
didn't understand the point
of commemorating any day
with flowers that were bound to die.

Today, with the groceries, you bring home
twenty-one delectable white roses,
each big as an infant's crown,
to mark the day I became a mother,
understanding, as women do,
the gift of temporal beauty.

The Passion

On Easter Eve, we see *Passion of the Christ*,
then afterwards, instead of necking in the car,
we fight our first fight, the kind with no topic.

I insist on being right about something,
while something for you just isn't fair.
Maybe those two somethings have something
in common—but for me it's a matter of my
intellectual property rights to the proper
New Testament story of Christ, in which Peter
denied Jesus and the cock crowed thrice.

I try to tell you Mel Gibson left the rooster out,
missed a moral nuance, but what I really mean is,
I was once born-again in a New Testament Church,
could spot the film-book deviations,
even tell you what was lost in translation,
after all, we read the goddamn bible in Greek,
though of course, Jesus himself spoke Aramaic
(one thing the film got right).

You aren't awed by my upper-room oration
so scales fall from your eyes, and you take up
your bed on the road to Damascus—no, you
don't give a damn about words, or roosters,
because the scars that run the length of your arms

in raised rivulets of flesh, had ached and twitched
as the Christ was given his stripes, in what for you
was more than a great make-up job.

You want to tell me you have known
the suffering that separates soul from flesh,
how cutting the body is transubstantiation,
a pain-numbing incarnation of agony,
so you interrupt my critique
of the Garden of Gethsemane scene,
with a raging primal scream—

and I tumble from my babbling tower,
lean (still buckled in) to kiss your cheek,
thinking, for the neighbor's sake,
it's a good thing the garage is six feet underground
and padded in concrete.

Behind us—the door thunders down.
A daughter, seeing the tomb-dark garage,
did a good deed. We gasp, burst into laughing tears,
escape our restraints, go inside the house
for wine, cheese and bread,
before playing Easter Rabbit for the kids,
then climbing naked into bed.

Ars Poetica

In my writing chair,
my back to the window,
      I marvel at the physics
of seeing you outdoors

reflected in my eyeglass lens,
your purple shirt an apparition
      as I angle my head,
here—gone,

your substance a mirage,
holding our dog
      in the right-angle of your arm,
reminding me of the time

I watched you play your oboe
in the medieval church gallery,
      I sat in the nave, gaze fixed
on your profile:

arms raised, mouth on reed,
enticing music to flow,
      a piece I still can't name
since I took no notes,

just sketched in my journal

with schoolgirl skill
        to capture your silhouette:
spiky hair, wide glasses,

sharp jaw, the slope of your breast
rising with each billowed breath,
        until the last lingering note
dispersed the image of you-as-instrument.

Now I glance up, see only
my tortoise shell frame.
        I look down at my blank page,
you reappear,
a hologram in glass periphery
        —here, gone—
I go on seeing

and unseeing you,
as I sit in my chair,
        not writing,
all I have is a glimpse,

not quite a vision,
more a guess, a wish,
        that it's you I see,
not a smudge on these glasses
I never get quite clean.

Crossing

I trace the swollen ridge
of scar along your arm,
as you tell of hiking up Kaiser Cairn,
following no road but your solace
through sylvan dark green.

You knelt on soft, brown needles
by a stream, drank the arctic current,
then took from rucksack
the knife you always carried
and slowly cut your arm,

then you rinsed the blade,
plunged the wound in icy water,
thrust aching wet fingers
into wool mittens you knit for yourself
in cream and gold
from an old Norwegian pattern.

The ribbed wrist held a wad of paper
against surging blood as you
sheathed knife, closed rucksack snaps,
turned your back to the mountain,
meandered through trees
toward town and the emergency
clinic on a pathless trail
that one day led to me.

Whole

neither of us gone,
no hole
in the day, or me

your medicine
and mine
waiting in two brass leaves
for us
and morning tea

two full cups
need four hands to steady
the brimming

yours is Darjeeling
and ginger,
mine milk-sweetened PG Tips,
steeped in cloves
and cardamom seeds

I watch you swallow
Eve's first draught

this is how we flow
between separate bodies:

two cups
on one table
together—each
also standing
alone

Rejuvenated

In the dream
you appear behind a red billowing sheet
I lift to show you
a hidden bed of anthurium heads:
red, huge, ripe, erect,
growing in a wealth of shadows.

"See what it wants
to show us," I say.

Embracing darkness,
we kiss like shadow puppets
on the sheet's screen.

I wake—4:45 am,
don't fall back to sleep.

At work, the first five people I meet
say I look beautiful.
Someone asks if I won a spa retreat.

Anniversary

one full year of
minutes
months
heartbeats
eye winks
snaps claps cloves
three-quarter time
whole notes
four-and-twenty
fortnights
afternoon rides
evening tides
sunrises mudslides
avalanches
riptides

fathoming
sounding
chorusing—*you-me*

when will love age,
mature, be full-grown,
resolute as stone—

not what we have,
but all we are

The Tuner

Your ear
pitch-perfect, hears
a tone, a chord,
disharmony, dissonance,
strain,
       even my pain,
self-pity, fear,
resignation,
accusation,
       a sigh
before it is mouthed,

the way music
begins with thought,
then feeling,
then voice,
       the will to speak,
or refrain,

silence, too, a symphony
in which you
distinguish
each instrument,
       reach in
with a stroke
or bit of pressure,

nimble fingers
on stops and frets,

warm breath
a moistening kiss,
filling hollows,
resolving discord,
aligning tone,
attunement.

Currents

When you hand me a handle-less teacup
with blue porcelain flowers, I think of my mother
saying science believed there was no such thing
as a blue flower, so if I found one, I'd be famous.

I looked for years, certain I'd seen one,
wondering if science had heard of bluebells.
In the end, I thought blue must be like apples.
Who could say if apple in my mouth
tasted apple to others?

You dip a wrought-iron spoon into the cup,
"Red currants, want some?"

I expect sweet—get Wisconsin summer breeze,
my grandma's clapboard house, white-petal-clouds
in a robin-egg-sky, a hedge higher than my head,
fat currants red-jeweling in leprechaun leaves,
my tongue pressing the berries, juice zapping electric—
red, the only flavor tasting only of itself.

I was a girl then, couldn't see over the hedge,
or dream I'd ever taste such juice again.

BLUE LIKE APPLES

POETRY BY RASMA HAIDRI

Blue Like Apples is a narrative collection of poems that tells a story of coming-out, through love for another woman. It is a coming of age in mid-life, after having never really discovered herself before during her long heterosexual marriage. It's the story of a marriage of minds and bodies that began in 2003 on the eve of the US invasion of Iraq, in a city in the Norwegian Arctic where they are both foreigners. The story doesn't end...

Rasma Haidri is a South Asian/Norwegian-American author of the poetry collection *As If Anything Can Happen* (Kelsay Books) and three ESL textbooks. She grew up in East Tennessee, spent formative years in Detroit, Miami, and Manhattan, studied in Wisconsin and France, and lived in Hawaii before moving permanently to Norway in 2001. She is currently the regional coordinator for the Norwegian Non-fiction Writers and Translators Association and serves on the fiction editorial board of PRISM International. Her poems and essays have been anthologized in the UK, USA, Canada, Norway, India, Israel, UAE, Pakistan, and Hong Kong, and appeared in literary magazines including *Prairie Schooner*, *River Teeth*, *Sycamore Review*, *Fourth Genre*, *I-70 Review*, *Muzzle Magazine* and *Under the Radar*. Recognitions for her writing include the Southern Women Writers Association creative non-fiction award, the Wisconsin Academy of Arts, Letters & Science poetry award, and a Best of the Net nomination from *NewVerseNews*. *Blue Like Apples* placed second in the BrickHouse Books' Wicked Woman Prize.

Visit her at www.rasma.org.

REBEL
SATORI
PRESS

INDEPENDENT PUBLISHERS ON THE FRONTIERS OF LIMINAL SPACE

ISBN 978-1-60864-276-2
51495
9 781608 642762